Decorative Braiding and Weaving

Decorative Braiding and Weaving

June Barker

Charles T Branford Company

Copyright © June Barker 1973
First published in the States 1973

Published in Great Britain 1973 by
B T Batsford Limited

Library of Congress Cataloging
Publication data:
Barker, June
Decorative Braiding and Weaving
1 Braid.   2 Hand weaving.   1 Title
TT 880.B3   746   72-10627
ISBN 1-8231-7031-4

Printed in Great Britain
for the publishers
Charles T Branford Company
28 Union Street, Newton Centre, Massachusetts 02159

Contents

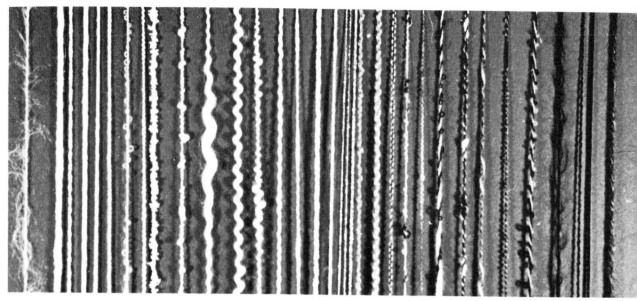

Figure 1 *(above)*

Figure 2 *(below)*

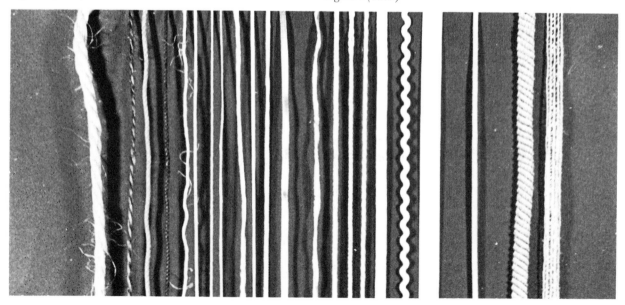

Introduction

A *braid* is a narrow strip of material which can be made by various textile construction techniques. A *plait* is the result of interlacing three or more lengths of yarn.

From the earliest times man has made braids for both functional and decorative purposes. The majority of textile construction techniques have evolved from working small areas of fabric, and similarly, braids are an excellent introduction to the textile construction crafts. No great physical strength is required for making braids. Some plaits and braids are simple enough for any child to work—but with variations, combinations and patterns, the work can be intricate enough to satisfy even the highly skilled worker. Most plaits and braids can be made with a minimum of equipment.

Textile construction can be divided roughly into two groups: those created with a continuous yarn, or those made with lengths of strands of yarn. Braids worked with a continuous yarn usually demand their own special equipment or tools—knitting needles, crochet hooks and hairpin forks. To construct braids from cut lengths of yarn, it is essential to calculate and control the lengths. The only reliable way to calculate the measurement of the various lengths for a plait or braid, is to work a small sample and from this, to estimate the amount required.

It is usual to work all the lengths taut, with one end firmly secured to withstand the pull of the worker. If there are only a small number of lengths, they can be knotted together, and the knot fastened to a hook or door knob. A greater number of lengths can be looped over a piece of string which is then tied between two supports. Or, similarly, the lengths can be arranged over a rod or pencil and trapped in a drawer. Alternatively, the lengths can be secured with pins at the top of a piece of pinboard and worked down the board.

If the lengths are extremely long or inclined to tangle, they can each be wrapped into small looped balls and secured with an elastic band. Otherwise, they may be wrapped around a small piece of card, the end being trapped in a slit at the side of the card, to prevent it from unwinding. As the work progresses, a small amount of yarn can be released at intervals.

When the braid has been completed the ends must be secured as invisibly as possible. Each plait and braid has its own problem which can only be solved with care and ingenuity. A hidden thread sewn through and across each end of the braid can be used successfully; another method is to hook back the ends into the reverse side of the braid.

Plaits and braids, as well as being complete in themselves, can be used to make fabrics. The separate braids can be joined together; some can be sewn, but others may be interlocked and joined during the working process. Fabric produced in this way will have a unique quality which cannot be produced by machine. If a braid is to be part of a fabric then it is better to avoid a heavy border design.

All yarns, cords, ribbons, tapes and strings—ranging from thickest to finest, the cheapest to the most expensive—are suitable for making braids, see figures 1 and 2. For some constructions it is advisable to use a certain type of yarn in order to learn the technique successfully. For example, rug wool is particularly suitable for beginners when learning to plait; the plait grows quickly and the structural form is clear and precise.

Once the construction techniques have been mastered, there is tremendous scope for the imaginative and creative use of all types of material.

1 Making simple cords

There are many ways of making a thicker, more attractive yarn or cord from a fine yarn, see figure 3.

TWISTED CORD

Take a length of fine yarn five times as long as the required cord and tie the lengths together. One end of the loop is placed around a hook or knob, and a pencil inserted into the other. Pull the loop taut. By twisting the pencil, the yarn will become twisted. When the yarn is well twisted, place the two ends of the loop together and the yarn will automatically twist itself into a four-ply cord. Secure the cord to prevent it from untwisting.

An attractive cord results if two different coloured lengths are used to form the initial loop.

CHAINED CORD

A chained cord can be worked with either the fingers or a crochet hook, using a continuous length of yarn. With a loop of yarn on the fingers or hook, draw through the free yarn to form a new loop, this is one chain. The action is repeated until you have the required length of cord. The end is then knotted.

Two different coloured yarns used to form alternate loops can produce a two-toned chained cord.

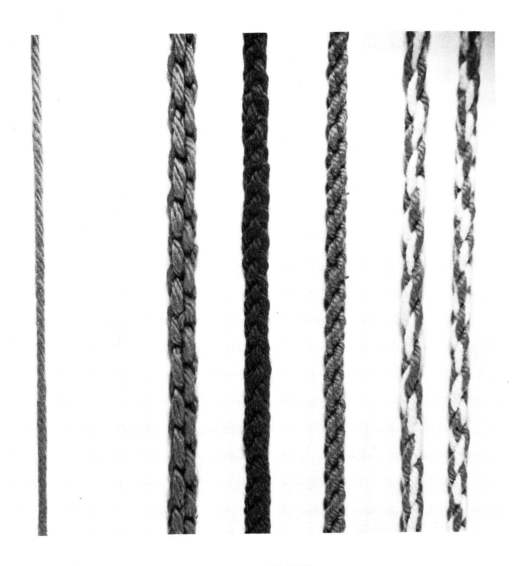

The three-stranded flat plait and the four-stranded rounded one can also be used as a method of making a thick yarn, see figures 4 and 40.

Figure 3

9

2 Plaited braids

Plaited braids are formed by three or more strands crossing each other diagonally, and, at the same time, passing over and under one another. The skill of plaiting is to use both hands equally efficiently. All plaits are constructed by working with the outer strands from both the left and right sides alternately. The plait is produced as the outer strands are worked to the centre.

The names of the plaits usually indicate the number of strands used in the construction. All plaited braids can be divided into two groups—flat and rounded.

FLAT PLAITS

The most familiar of all the flat plaits is the three-plait, associated with the plaiting and braiding of hair.

A three plait is made by working the outer strand into the centre, first from one side and then from the other, see figure 4. It is a narrow, but under-estimated braid.

Figure 4 Working pattern for the three plait:
3 strands A B C
C over B becomes A C B
A over C becomes C A B
B over A becomes C B A
C over B becomes B C A
A over C becomes B A C
B over A becomes A B C

Figure 5 *(left)*   Three plaits with beads and sequins

Figure 6 *(above)*   Three plaits with a variety of yarns

The three plait can be used as a thread and makes an interesting and personal yarn. Beads thread very easily onto one of the three strands and are fixed into position in the course of constructing the plait, see figure 5. For all hand weavers, the three plait can be used as a weft yarn for woven panels and wall hangings. Using different textured yarns in each strand of the three plait can be an exciting and stimulating introduction to plaiting, see figures 6–10. Plaiting *three* plaits together produces an intriguing larger braid, see figure 11.

Figure 7 *(far left)* Three plait with one thick and two thin yarns

Figure 8 *(left)* Three plait using textured yarn

Figure 9 *(above)* Variations of the three plait made by drawing up one of the three strands

Figure 10 *(above)*　Variations of the three plait
Figure 11 *(right)*　Three, three plaits worked together

The *four plait* uses a similar construction to the three plait, the only difference being that, from *one side only*, the outside thread passes over two strands to the centre.

A four plait can have a very distinctive pattern when two tones or colours are used. By arranging the threads in a different tone or colour sequence before working, two individually patterned plaits are constructed, as can be seen in figure 12.

Figure 12   Working pattern for the four plait:
4 strands A B C D
A over B C becomes B C A D
D over A becomes B C D A
B over C D becomes C D B A
A over B becomes C D A B
C over D A becomes D A C B
B over C becomes D A B C
D over A B becomes A B D C
C over D becomes A B C D

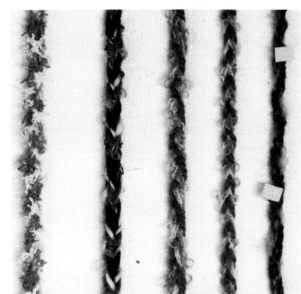

Figure 13 *(above left)*   Four plait

Figure 14 *(above right)*   Four plait

Figure 15 *(above far right)*   Four plaits, flat and rounded

Figure 16 *(right)*   Variations of the four plait

Five and seven plaits can be worked using the same construction—the outer strands always passing over *half* the number of threads to the centre.

As the number of threads increases, the braids become less firm. Distinctive patterns result when two tones or colours are chosen, dividing the strands into two groups (as shown in figure 17 with the seven plait).

All the plaits described so far have the same basic construction, i.e. passing the outer strands in one movement to the centre. To work a plaited braid with a large number of strands, the outer thread must be darned, or woven under and over the adjacent threads, before reaching the centre. This gives a firm, solid and flat construction to the braid.

The odd-numbered plait is the most versatile. That is, one worked with any odd number of strands. Figure 18 shows the plait constructed with five strands. This is made by dividing the groups of threads into two half-groups, trying to keep the threads lying flat and in sequence.

As this plait is always worked with an odd number of strands, one half-group always has an extra thread, see figures 19–21. Hold the larger group in the left hand. Working with the outside thread of the left-hand group, weave it under and over the adjacent strands to the centre, to join the group held in the right hand. The same action is then worked with the right-hand group. The plait is constructed as these two actions are repeated.

A B C D E F G

Figure 17 Seven plait

A B C D E

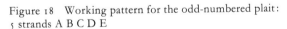

Figure 18 Working pattern for the odd-numbered plait:
5 strands A B C D E
A over B under C becomes B C A D E
E over D under A becomes B C E A D
B over C under E becomes C E B A D
D over A under B becomes C E D B A
C over E under D becomes E D C B A
A over B under C becomes E D A C B
E over D under A becomes D A E C B
B over C under E becomes D A B E C
D over A under B becomes A B D E C
C over E under D becomes A B C D E

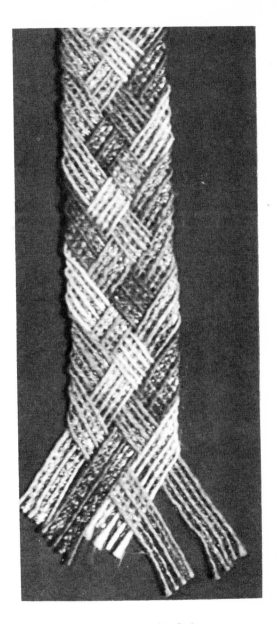

Figure 19 Odd-numbered plait worked in *Juvisca*

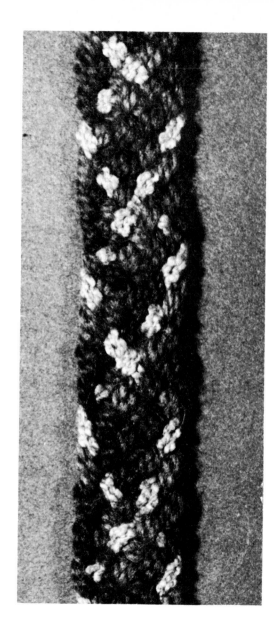

Figure 20   Odd-numbered plait worked in tape

Figure 21   Odd-numbered plait worked in double wool yarn

The even-numbered plait has quite a different character, although it has the same basic structure. All the strands are grouped and held together and only the outside left strand is worked. This strand weaves under and over all the remaining strands to the right-hand side, see figure 22. The angle of the diagonal gives the braid its characteristic appearance. This plait can be worked with both a slack and tight tension and the resulting plaits look very different from one another.

All plaits constructed by means of the weaving or darning technique are capable of many variations. These are made by altering the number of strands that are woven over or under.

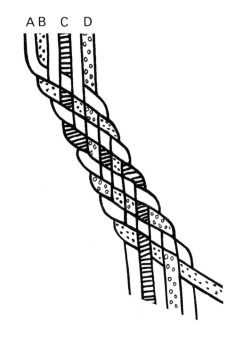

Figure 22   Even-numbered plait

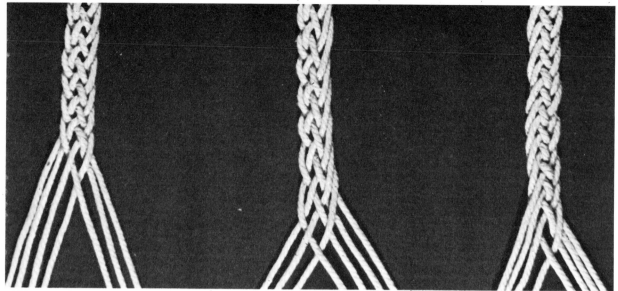

Figures 23 and 24 *(above and below)* Flat plaits with a variety of strands worked in string

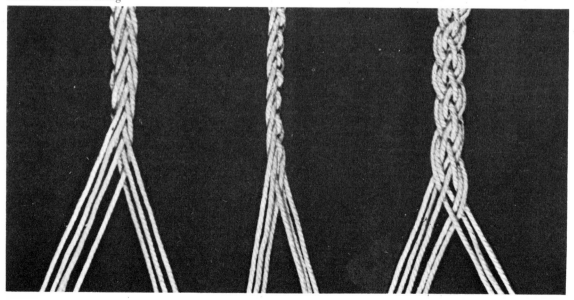

A diagonal striped braid can be constructed with a four plait. The two pairs of coloured threads are arranged with the outer strands in the second colour, see figure 25. The outside *left* thread passes over one strand towards the centre; the outside *right* thread passes under a strand and over a strand towards the centre. These two actions are repeated alternately until the plait is complete.

A B C D

Figure 25   Working pattern for a diagonal-striped four plait:
4 strands A B C D
A over B becomes B A C D
D under C over A becomes B D A C
B over D becomes D B A C
C under A over B becomes D C B A
D over C becomes C D B A
A under B over D becomes C A D B
C over A becomes A C D B
B under D over C becomes A B C D

Figures 26 and 27 *(left and above)*   Diagonal-striped four plaits

The following are some of the many variations of plaiting:

1 Six plait, held in two even groups and worked from the left-hand side under two strands; and from the right-hand side over two strands and under one.

2 Six plait, held in two even groups and worked from the left-hand side under one strand and over one; and from the right-hand side under one strand and over two.

3 Seven plait, grouped with four strands in the left hand and worked from the left-hand and right-hand sides alternately over two strands and under one.

4 Seven plait, grouped with five strands in the left hand and worked from the left-hand side under one and over one; and from the right-hand side over three strands and under one.

5 Eight plait, grouped with five strands in the left hand and worked from the left-hand side under three strands and over one; and from the right-hand side over three strands.

6 Eight plait, grouped with five strands in the left hand and worked with the two outside strands, over two strands and under one from each side alternately.

As well as being constructed with different threads, these plaits can easily be worked in tapes, ribbons, or a combination of both. A piece of soft board and pins can be a great help in controlling the construction of plaits when using a large number of strands.

Figure 28 Plait with an even number of strands

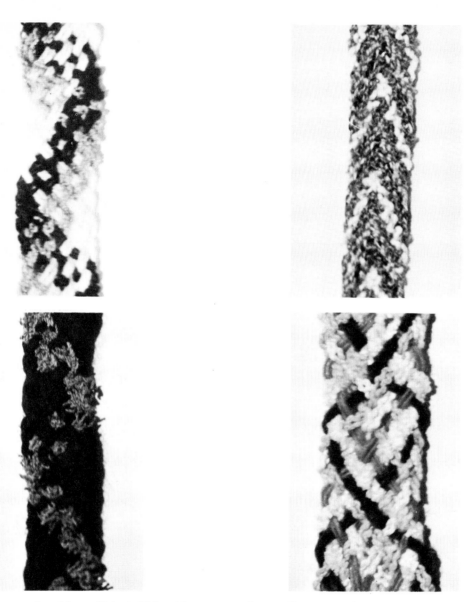

Figures 29 and 30 *(above and below)* Plaits with an even number of strands

Figures 31 and 32 *(above and below)* Plaits with an odd number of strands

Figures 33, 34, 35 and 36 Variations on plaits with many strands

A B C D

The *zigzag plait* requires a piece of soft board and pins for its construction. These are essential for controlling the angles and assist in keeping the edges straight. The zigzag plait can be made in any number of strands, from three to twelve. The greater the number of strands, the less firm the resulting braid. One length of the zigzag plait positioned near the centre is never worked, but remains vertically down the middle of the plait. The other strands weave under and over horizontally from one side to the other, see figure 37.

Figure 38 *(opposite)*   Zigzag plaits worked in *Juvisca*

Figure 39 *(overleaf)*   Zigzag plaits

Figure 37   Zigzag plait

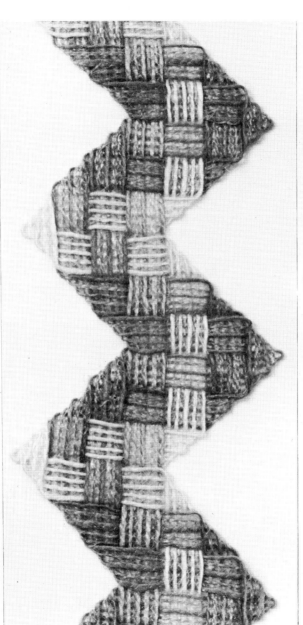

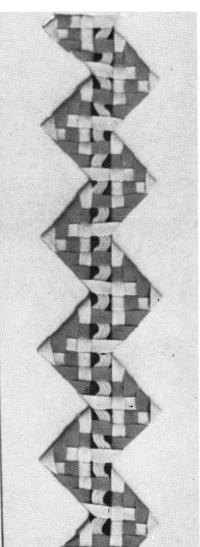

A B C D

The simplest of all the rounded plaits is the one constructed with four strands.

A four plait can be made of lengths of single thread, or a group of finer threads held together as one. In order to become familiar with the rhythm of the plaited construction, it is easier to work with two colours grouped in pairs, see figure 40.

Hold one pair of threads in the left hand and the other pair in the right. The plait is worked by taking the outside thread in the left-hand group behind two threads and up between the pair of threads held in the right hand, then back over one thread to rest in the left hand again.

This action is then repeated, using the outside right-hand thread. Both actions are then worked alternately. Once the technique is mastered, this plait can be made as quickly as the more familiar three-stranded flat plait.

Figure 40 Working pattern for a rounded four plait:
4 strands A B C D
A behind B C over C becomes B A C D
D behind C A over A becomes B A D C
B behind A D over D becomes A B D C
C behind D B over B becomes A B C D

Figures 41, 42, 43 and 44 *(opposite)* Rounded four plaits using a variety of materials including textured yarns and beads

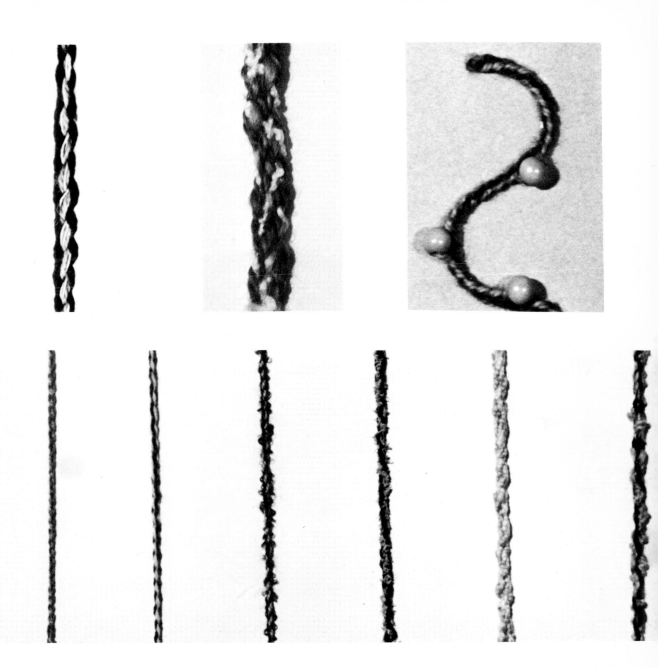

For much thicker rounded plaits, the same construction is employed, but always with an even number of strands.

An eight-stranded round plait can be worked by passing the outer thread behind five strands in one direction, then over two in the opposite direction, to rest always in its own group. A thick, chunky chevron pattern is produced when the eight strands are arranged in a colour sequence, see figure 45. By changing the colour sequence, or by using only two or three different ones, many different patterns can be made.

A five-stranded round plait is made by dividing the strands into two groups, with three strands held in the left hand and the other two in the right. Working with the outside left strand, pass under two strands and over one. With the outside right strand, pass under three strands and over one. These two actions are worked alternately.

Another eight-stranded round plait is made by dividing the strands into two equal groups, one in each hand. Taking the outside left strand, pass behind four strands to the right, and then back to the left over one strand. This action is worked from both sides alternately.

The last two rounded plaits look better when made in a single colour, for this shows their relief and construction to advantage.

Figure 45   Working pattern for a rounded eight plait:
8 strands A B C D E F G H
A behind B C D E F over F E becomes B C D A   E F G H
H behind G F E A D over D A becomes B C D A   H E F G
B behind C D A H E over E H becomes C D A B   H E F G
G behind F E H B A over A B becomes C D A B   G H E F
C behind D A B G H over H G becomes D A B C   G H E F
F behind E H G C B over B C becomes D A B C   F G H E
D behind A B C F G over G F becomes A B C D   F G H E
E behind H G F D C over C D becomes A B C D   E F G H

Figure 46 *(opposite above)*   Rounded plaits, variations worked in string

Figure 47 *(opposite below)*   Eight-stranded round plait

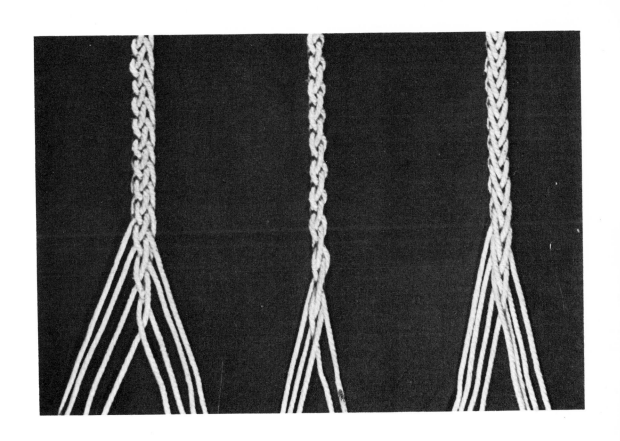

Figure 48 *(above)* Fabric made from many strands of flat plaiting by Jill Monk

Figure 49 *(below)* Fabric made from plaiting by Jan Mansell

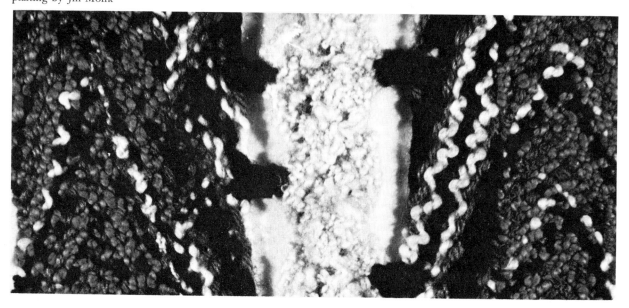

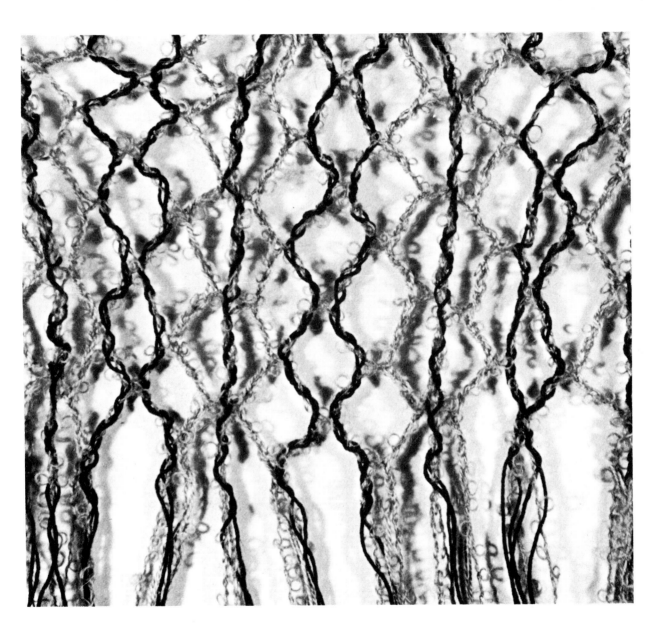

Figure 50   Three plait fabric by Jackie Duffield

Figure 51 *(opposite)*   Fabric made of various plaits

Figure 52   Wall hanging by June Barker

3 Tablet woven braids

Tablet, or card weaving is one of the oldest techniques for constructing a narrow strip of fabric, a braid. As the name suggests, the construction involves the use of a set of cards or tablets.

THE TABLETS

These can be made of heavy card, wood, metal or plastic. They must be thin, smooth and strong. Those in general use are 5 cm (2 in.) plastic squares, rounded at the corners with a hole in each corner. Other tablets of different shapes can be used, see figure 53. This shows a narrow rectangle with two holes; a triangle with a hole at each angle; and even more complex tablets of hexagonal or octagonal shape, with six or eight holes (the latter being used only for very complicated patterns).

The holes should be numbered on one side of each tablet to help with threading. A length of yarn is threaded through each hole. The width of the braid depends upon the number of tablets used and the thickness of the yarn chosen. More tablets have to be used if the yarn is very fine.

THE YARN

Yarns for tablet weaving must be strong, well twisted and fairly smooth. Wool can be a very frustrating yarn to use, as it fluffs easily and may even wear through as the weaving proceeds. Cotton yarns, the thickness of three-ply wool, and no more than twelve tablets are quite adequate for the beginner.

For each square tablet there are four lengths of yarn, each length should be one and a half times the required length of the finished braid. So there will be forty-eight lengths of yarn if twelve square tablets are used. These are the warp or foundation threads and will be seen in the finished braid. However, each tablet is responsible for only one warp thread thickness in the width of the finished braid.

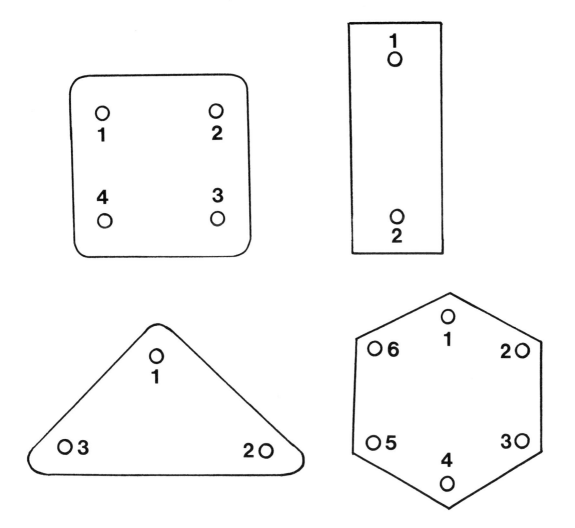

Figure 53

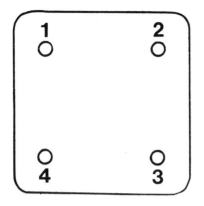

PATTERN

The construction of tablet woven braids is very distinctive, as the threads through each tablet are plyed or twisted into vertical columns. The number of twisted columns in a braid indicate the number of tablets used. One tablet, threaded with four lengths of the same colour, will yield a column of that colour. Another tablet threaded with four different colours will produce a column with the four colours plied in sequence.

All basic patterns in tablet weaving are planned in the threading of the tablets, although intriguing variations can be made in the actual weaving. The easiest way to plan a pattern is to use squared paper, see figure 54. Four vertical squares represent the four holes in the square tablet; and the number of horizontal squares indicate the number of tablets required. Figures 55–58 show further examples of this planning method, and the resulting braids.

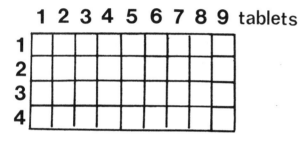

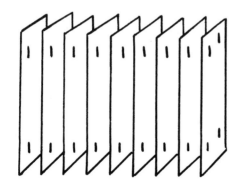

Figure 54

Figure 55 *(opposite)* Example of a pattern worked out on squared paper and the braid produced:
a Pattern; b Decorative end of braid; c Reverse side

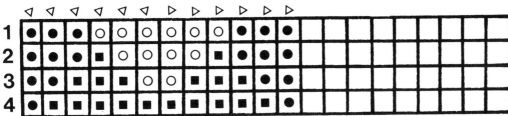

KEY: ○ goldfingering ■ white ● black ▲ pink

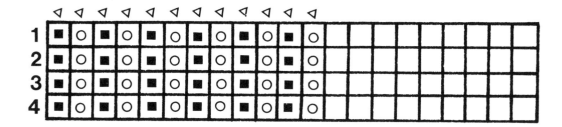

Figure 56 *(opposite above)* Example of a pattern on squared paper and the braid produced:
a Threads used are gold fingering, white, black and pink

Figure 57 *(opposite below)* Another example of the same technique

Figure 58 *(above)* A further example

The measured lengths of yarn, the warp, should be arranged in sequence, according to the threading pattern, on a thick piece of string or rod, see figure 59. The lengths should also be grouped and secured in some way to prevent tangling until they are needed for threading through the tablets. A chain or thread holding the warp in groups of four, see figure 60, can be a great help and time-saver.

If only a small sample is needed, then it is often as quick to measure the length of yarn and to thread it through the tablet straight away.

Lay the grouped warp threads flat on a table. Each single thread in a group is then threaded through one hole in a tablet, according to the threading pattern. All four threads for the same tablet should be threaded in the same direction, i.e. from the numbered side of the tablet to the blank side.

In some diagonal patterned braids, the threading of half the pattern is reversed. This is usually indicated in the threading draft by an arrow, see figure 61.

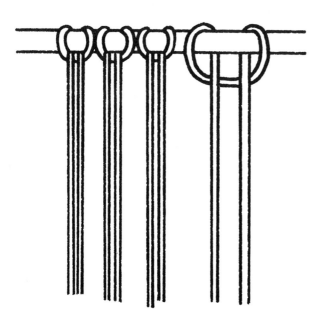

Figure 59

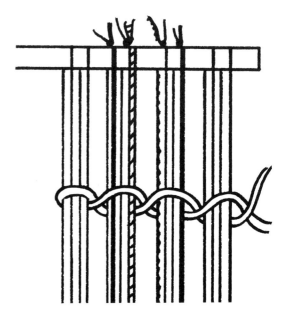

Figure 60

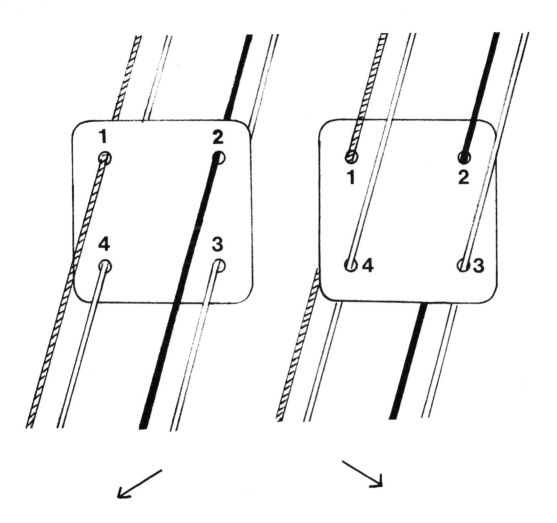

Figure 61

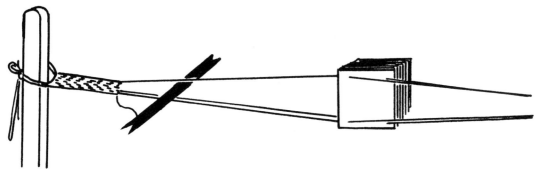

Figure 62

When all the tablets are threaded, the numbered sides are arranged to face in the same direction and in the same number sequence. The tablets are then slipped along the warp threads to within 35 cm (12 in.) from the end, where the weaving is to take place, see figure 62.

The warp threads must be kept taut during weaving. If the threads are arranged on a rod, this can be closed in a drawer. If they are on a string, this may be tied to a door knob or hook, or between two vertical supports (two legs of an upturned chair, for instance). The other ends should be tied in a group to the back of the weaver's chair, or to a belt around the weaver's waist. The tighter and more secure the warp threads, the easier it is to weave the braid.

The weft or binding thread in tablet weaving must be very strong. It is seen only at the outside edges of the finished braid, so the colour chosen must be one of the colours used in the threading up of the first or last tablet. If the braid is to have a border, then these two tablets will both be threaded with the same coloured yarn, and this colour should also be used for the weft.

As the warp threads are held as tight as possible, they divide themselves into two groups near the tablets. This is the opening or *shed* for the weft thread. By twisting the tablets one quarter turn, a new shed is formed for the weft, as indicated in figure 63. At each quarter turn, the weft thread passes through the opening in alternate directions. The weaver must check, after each quarter turn, that every tablet has turned, the numbers make this quite easy. It can be an advantage to colour the sides of home-made tablets, as well as numbering the holes— e.g. colour the edges between numbers 1 and 2 red, between 2 and 3 green, and so on—so the weaver can see immediately if any one of the tablets is out of step.

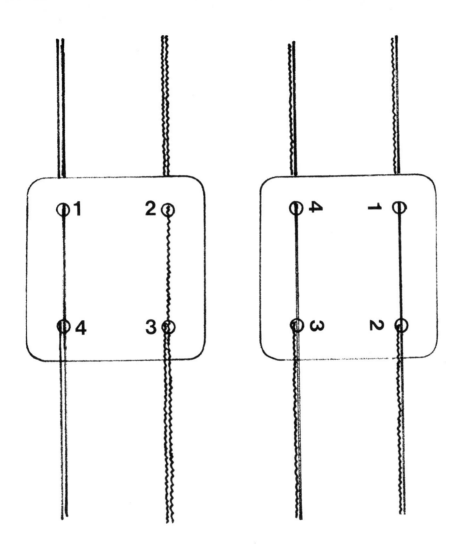

Figure 63

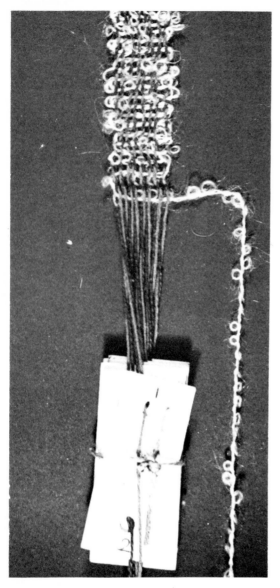

Figure 64 The tablets are tied into a bundle when there is a pause in work. Two-holed rectangular tablets and *Leno* braid

If the threads are catching on one another, run your finger along the shed to check that for each tablet there are two threads at the top of the opening shed, and two at the bottom. Turning the tablets can be awkward at first, but it becomes easier with practice, especially if the weaver slides the tablets gently up and down the warp and does not press them too close together.

As a tablet-woven braid is a warp-patterned braid, the weft thread must be drawn tight enough to bring the warp threads close together. The weft yarn should be pushed or beaten firmly into position to give the braid a firm construction, and pulled up to a correct tension to give the braid an even width with firm edges.

SEQUENCE OF TURNS

As the braid is constructed with the tablets turning in one direction only, and as the threads below the tablets also twist, these must be periodically un-ravelled. This need not happen if the braid is constructed by turning the tablets a certain number of quarter turns in one direction, then reversing the direction for an equal number of turns.

It is important to remember or record the sequence of turns and here the numbers on the tablets are a great help. By changing the direction in which the tablets are turned (clockwise or anti-clockwise; one, two, three, four or four, three, two, one) the arrange-ments of the plyed threads are altered, often producing quite a different pattern. If the sequences are very short, the braid may develop uneven edges. This can be corrected if the border tablets are always kept turning in the same direction, or by threading the border tablets in the opposite direction to the others.

Inkle loom braids ▶

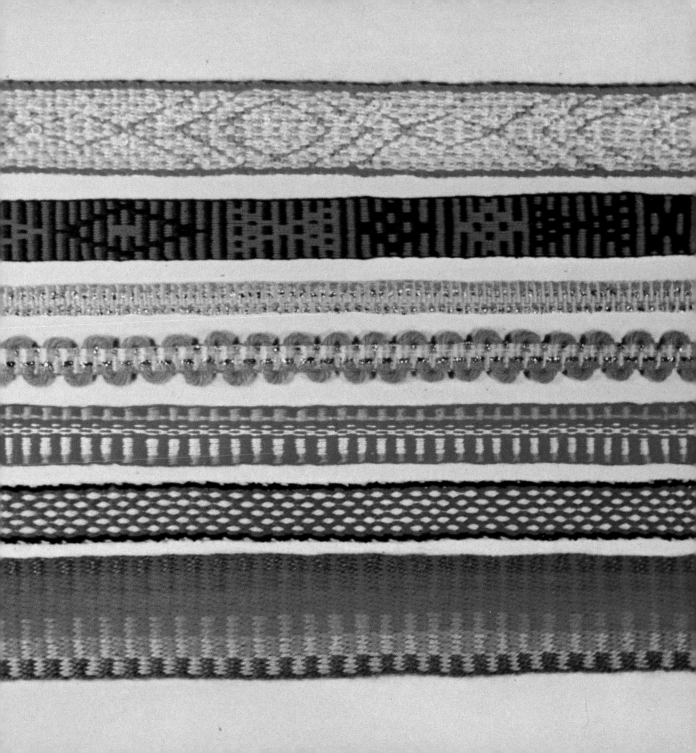

Should you stop work before the braid is complete, slide the tablets up to the woven section of the braid and secure them with an elastic band or piece of string. Tie up the tablets like a parcel, see figure 64. This prevents a lot of confusion when work is resumed. A pencil or stick, placed through the central hole which some tablets have, keeps the tablets in sequence when not in use.

VARIATIONS

1 Weaving with hexagonal tablets gives a choice of two or three sheds. The warp threads can divide themselves into three groups at each turn. The weft is worked from one side of the braid only, passing through one shed, right to left, and back again through the other shed, left to right. Alternatively, the weaver can work with two weft threads. The centre group of warp threads can be bound into the middle of the braid, resulting in a thicker and very strong braid.

2 The square tablets can be used in this way, using the rounded corners as the highest and lowest points.

3 A *leno* (net) or gauze construction can be made by using two-holed rectangular tablets, see figure 64.

Figure 65 Cardboard tablets

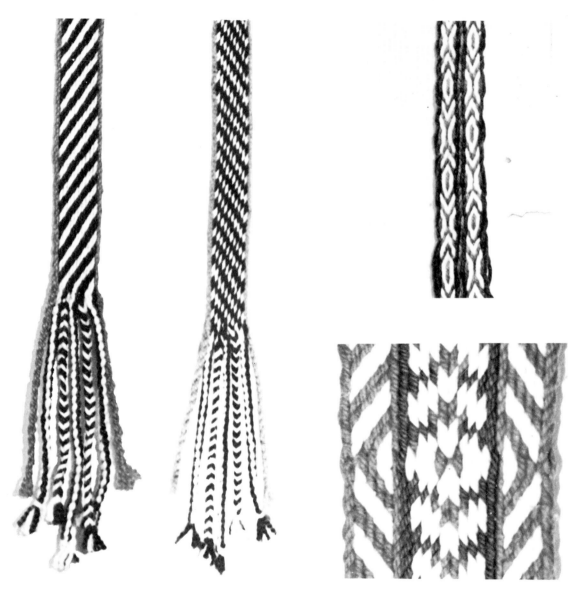

Figure 66a *(left)* Right side of braid, ends plaited
Figure 66b *(right)* Reverse side of braid

Figure 67 *(above)* Braid
Figure 68a *(below)* Detail of plaiting

Figure 68b   Plaiting in tablet weaving

Figure 69   Decorative wefts, four strands of black mohair, and beads

4 *Inkle loom braids*

Inkle loom braids are made on an Inkle loom. The exact origin of these looms is unknown, but the name Inkle is given to narrow woven tapes. Inkle looms have been in use in England and Scotland for the past three hundred years.

THE LOOM

This is very simple, easy to thread up and easy to weave upon. There are various designs, the most common is the one shown in figure 70. This floor-standing loom is made of wood and is approximately 92 cm (3 ft) high.

There are many other designs, like the one shown in figure 71, some of which can be made at home quite easily with little carpentry skill.

The Inkle loom should be very sturdy, since the pressure of threads can be great when weaving.
Leash pegs can be purchased separately, or they too can be made at home, using stout cord twisted around a peg. At every other twist, a long loop measuring 152 mm (6 in.) is left; or the loops can be formed as shown in figure 72. For every 25 mm (1 in.) of peg there should be approximately five loops. The usual number of leash loops per peg is twenty-four, all the same length and very firmly secured to the peg. This is done with a spot of glue on each knot.

An Inkle loom braid is a warp patterned braid, i.e. the yarns used in threading up the loom are those visible in the finished braid. The length of the braid is calculated around the pegs of the loom.

The shortest length is made by threading around pegs A, B, C, A. The longest length is made by threading around pegs A, B, D, C, E, A. Pegs D and E are adjustable so that the weaver can organize the length of braid required.

There are always about 200 mm (8 in.) left at the extreme end of the warp which it is impossible to weave. It is also usual to lose approximately 50 mm in every 305 mm (2 in. in every foot) of the warp length due to shrinkage; this is because the construction take-up of the braid is all in the warp. These last two points must always be remembered in calculating the length of the warp.

It is important always to include peg C which adjusts the warp tension after threading is completed and as the woven construction takes place.

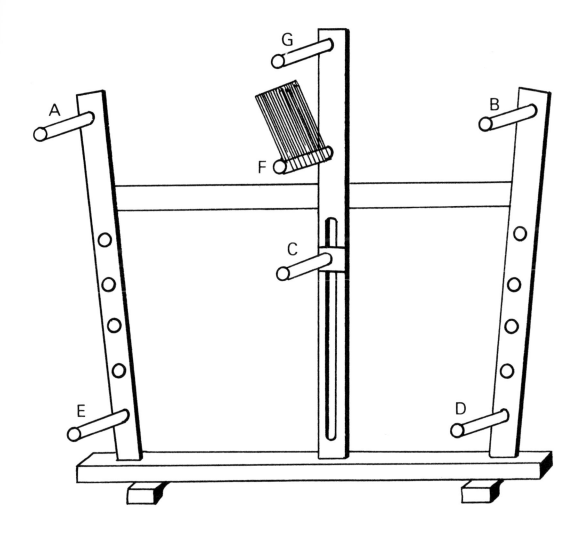

Figure 70 The Inkle loom. The following two routes are used alternately to thread up the loom:
A B C and back to A
A, through a loop of the leash peg F, over G B C and back to A

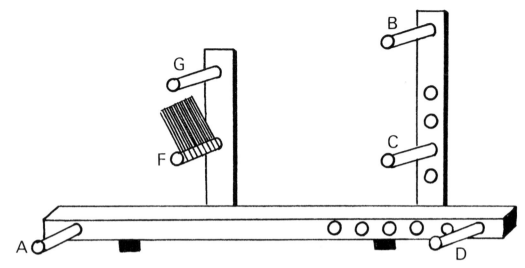

Figure 71   An Inkle loom like this could easily be made at home

THREADING UP

This is a simple procedure. All the threads must go around the loom using the appropriate pegs for the length of braid required. The knots to join one thread to the next choice of thread must be made at peg A. Never tie a knot to the peg, but tie it to itself or an adjacent thread.

Every alternate thread must be threaded through a loop of the leash peg F and over the peg G directly above it, before continuing the circuit back to peg A.

The following two routes are used alternately to thread up the loom:
A, B, C and back to A
A, through a loop of the leash peg F, over G, B, C and back to A

It is usual to use all the loops of the leash pegs, unless a very narrow braid is desired.

METHOD OF WORKING

All the warp threads should be taut and have an even tension. The weaving of the braid takes place between pegs A and the parallel pegs G and F. The weaver sits comfortably in a position at the left-hand end of the loom.

By placing the hand behind the leash loops, the lower half of the warp can be pulled up or pushed down, so making two different sheds for the weft or binding yarn. The two sheds are used alternately to pass the weft horizontally through the warp.

The weft or binding yarn should be very strong, as it draws the warp threads close together, being seen only at the outside edges of the braid. The width of the Inkle braid is controlled by the pull of the weft yarn, and the density by the pressure exerted to beat the weft into place. A small piece of card or a template can help the beginner to keep an even width.

Figure 72

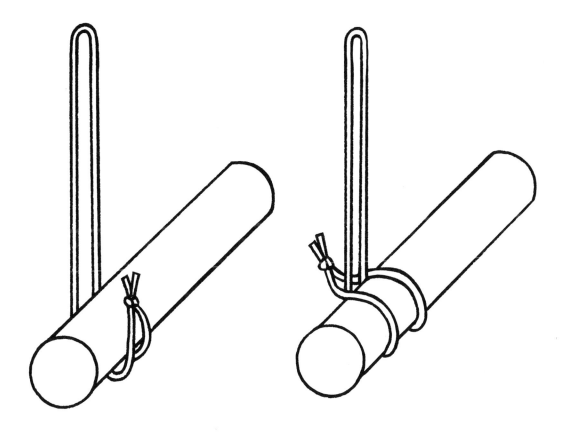

Periodic adjustment of peg C should ensure that the warp remains at an even tension. Since the braid is woven only between peg A and the leash peg, it is necessary at intervals to pull the warp around the loom to the weaving position, until the braid is completed.

YARNS

Most yarns are suitable for Inkle loom braids, provided that they are fairly strong. Textured yarns should be handled with care and if possible, threaded in the straight section of the warp, to avoid rubbing when the warp is pulled around the loom.

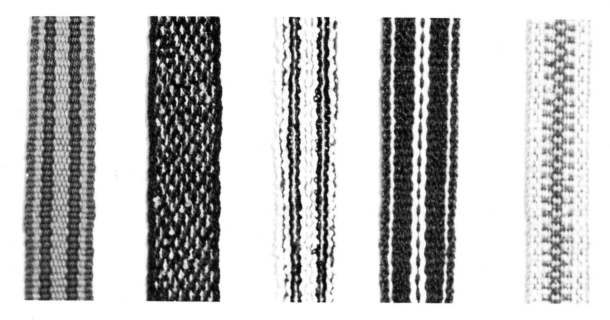

Figure 73

PATTERNS

The variety of patterns produced by Inkle weaving is endless, see figure 73. The warp is often arranged in stripes. A border for a braid is made by threading the first and last two, four or six threads in the same yarn.

1 Vertical stripes are produced by threading two or four threads of the same colour next to one another, see figure 74.

2 For horizontal stripes, two different coloured yarns are threaded alternately: one colour in the straight section of the warp and the other threaded through the leash loops. By carrying small bundles of each coloured yarn in sequence around the loom for the whole of the warp threading, the loom can be put to work very much more quickly.

3 Chain designs are made by three adjacent warp threads, the centre thread being a contrast in colour, tone or texture to the other two. Double chain designs are made by five warp threads, the centre thread being the contrasting one.

4 A repeating sequence of five different coloured threads can produce a fascinating chequered effect.

5 Other variations in plain woven Inkle braids can be made by varying the thickness of the weft yarn. If two wefts, one thick, one fine, are used alternately, the resulting braid has a ribbed texture or effect.

6 Two weft threads used as one can be made to produce a fringed braid. One weft is employed in the construction of the braid itself; the other, decorative weft is wrapped around a pencil or piece of card at the edge of the weaving to make a loop. This loop can be left double, or the ends cut, making a decorative fringed edging to the braid.

The Inkle loom can also be used to make braids with more complicated weaves and patterns. Some of these require special threading sequences for the warp and more time and skill in the weaving.

1   When the loom is threaded throughout with the same coloured yarn, a pattern can be made by passing the weft thread over certain warp threads. The weft yarn should be thicker, and in a contrasting colour to the warp, in order to make a distinctive pattern.

2   If, alternatively, the loom is threaded with an uneven number of light-coloured yarns through all the leash loops, and an uneven number of dark-coloured yarns for the straight section of the warp, patterns can be made by picking up and holding certain dark threads above the lighter half of the warp. Pick up the desired threads from in front of the leash loops. If the darker yarn is slightly thicker than the lighter one, the pattern produced will be more pronounced.

Figure 74

Pick-up patterns must be carefully centred, and each pick-up thread counted according to the desired pattern. Patterns are best designed on squared paper; one square to represent one warp thread, and each row of squares represents half the warp, as the seen in the woven braid.

A stick, pencil or knitting needle helps to hold up the pattern threads. After a little practice this becomes much easier and quicker. Picking up the pattern threads is made less difficult on the push-down shed with the weft thread working horizontally, right to left. The pull-up shed is always woven plain.

In patterned weaves, the weft thread must not be pulled too tight. This can often destroy an interesting texture on the surface of the braid.

The variations of Inkle loom braids, both with plain and patterned weave, are unlimited. They are both fascinating to look at and to make, see figures 75–78.

Figure 75 *(above)*

Figure 76 *(right)*   Detail of a rug made from Inkle loom strips sewn together. The strips were worked in six-ply rug wool

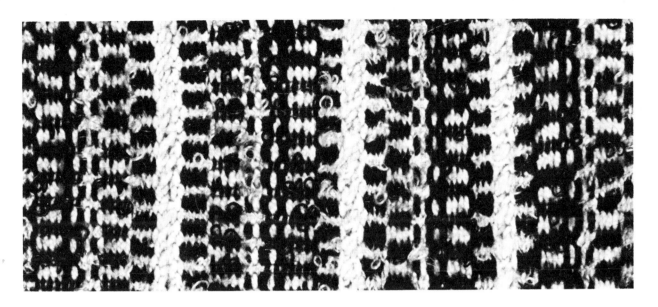

Figure 77 *(above)* Fabric made from Inkle loom woven strips sewn together

Figure 78 *(below)* A section of fabric worked by Jo Silverthorn. Inkle loom braids are joined together with a central knotted section

5 Crochet braids

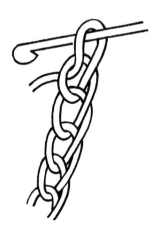

Figure 79   The crochet chain

Crochet braids are narrow strips of crochet work. Crochet is a looping construction like knitting, but is worked with a hook. The loops are made one at a time with a continuous length of yarn. A single chain can be worked with the fingers alone, but for more elaborate work, a hook is essential.

Hooks vary in thickness depending on the yarn to be used. They may be bought, or made out of dowelling, but this is suitable for coarse work only, using fairly thick yarn or string. For finer work, use a smooth metal hook. The hook is held in the same way as holding a pencil, and it is the hook which is pivoted around to take up the loose thread, held and stretched between the thumb and index finger of the other hand.

All crochet stitches are based upon variations of the single chain. There is no need to learn all the very elaborate and complicated stitches to produce simple and attractive braids.

The following stitches are the most versatile and useful ones for the beginner. For more advanced work, any crochet manual will have a full and comprehensive list.

THE CHAIN

A crochet chain, see figure 79, is worked by making a slip knot in the yarn which forms a loop on the hook. Catch the yarn with the hook and draw it through the loop. This is one chain. Repeated through every new loop formed on the hook, a chain results.

Variations on the chain construction can be made by working with two yarns; either of contrasting colours or with different textures. A chain stitch is constructed first in one yarn, and then with another. An interesting narrow braid results when the chain is worked in a fine yarn around a thicker thread.

All the other stitches are worked on a chain foundation which can be either the width or the length of the braid.

DOUBLE CROCHET

Work a chain of the required length, see figure 80, and then turn back along it. Insert the hook into a chain and draw the yarn through. There are now two loops on the hook. Pick up another loop from the yarn and draw it through these two loops, leaving one new loop on the hook to repeat the process.

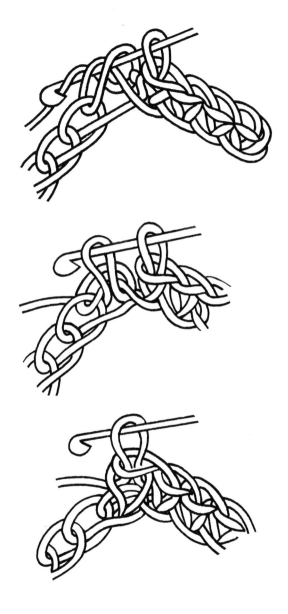

Figure 80 Double crochet

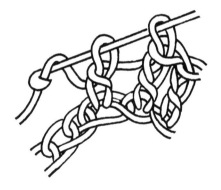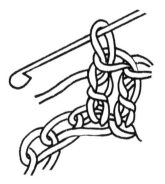

Figure 81   Treble crochet

TREBLE CROCHET

Trebles, see figures 81, 82 and 83, form little columns or bars. With a chain of the desired length already worked, place the yarn over the hook, making two loops on the hook. Insert the hook into a chain, then draw up a third loop onto the hook. Place the yarn over the hook to make another loop and then draw that through two of the loops on the hook. Place the yarn over the hook again, and draw it through the two remaining loops on the hook. Leave one new loop on the hook to repeat the process for the next treble.

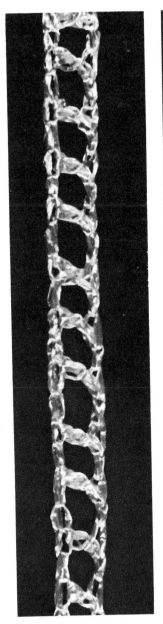

Figure 82 *(left)* Treble crochet braid worked in raffia

Figure 83 *(right)* Treble crochet braid worked in raffia with a satin ribbon threaded along it

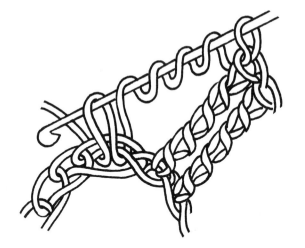

Trebles are the most versatile of all crochet stitches:
1 The simplest variation can be made by wrapping the yarn around the hook before inserting it into the chain. A double treble has two wrapped loops; a triple treble has three; a quadruple treble has four. See figures 84 and 85. But the drawing-through action is confined to two loops at a time as in the basic treble construction; and so the column character is retained, only lengthened.
2 Treble columns can be spaced out, remembering to work the same number of chains after a completed treble as every chain interval missed, see figure 86.
3 Clusters can be made using the treble construction. The last loop of each treble is retained on the hook until a required number of closely-worked trebles have been made. The last loop is then drawn through all the retained loops on the hook, thus forming a group or cluster, see figure 87.
4 A distinctive wrapped column is constructed when the pick-up loop is drawn through all the wrapped loops in one action, see figure 88. This stitch is most attractive when worked with a large number of wrapped loops on the hook. However it should be attempted only with a yarn such as wool, which has some elasticity.

Figure 84 *(above)*   Double treble

Figure 85 *(below)*   Quadruple treble

64

Figure 86   Spaced treble

Figure 87   Clusters

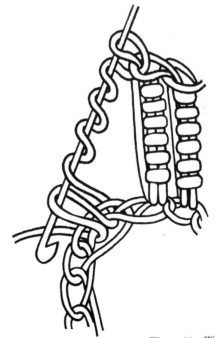

◀ Fabric constructed from a series of plaits

Figure 88   Wrapped trebles

Long narrow crochet braids look better when the foundation chain is central in the braid. This is easily managed by working into the chain first from one edge, then working the same stitch or number of rows from the other edge of the chain, see figure 89.

If beads are required in a crochet braid they must be threaded onto the yarn in sequence, if more than one colour is to be used, before the work commences. As the work proceeds, the beads can be slipped up the yarn into position, so becoming an integral part of the design and construction of the braid, see figure 90.

Figure 89 *(above)*

Figure 90 *(right)*   Crochet edging worked in tape with wooden beads

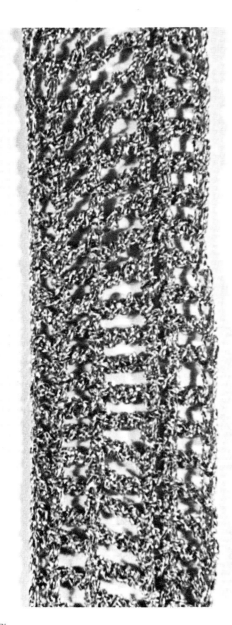

Figure 91

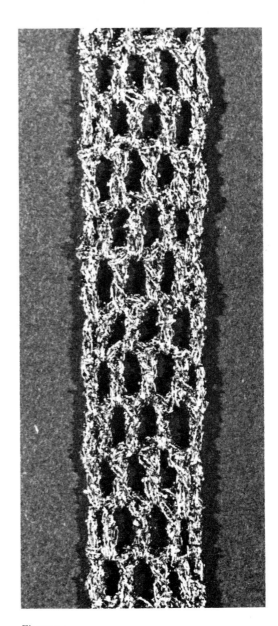

Figure 92

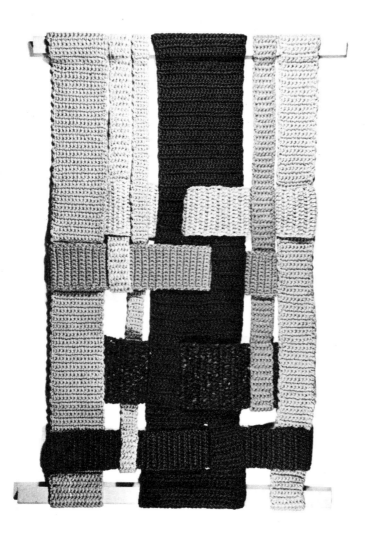

Figure 93   Wall hanging 508 mm × 1016 mm (20 in. × 40 in.)
by Vicki Buckton, made of pink, orange and purple crochet
braids

6 Hairpin crochet

Hairpin crochet is a most attractive looped crochet braid, constructed around a metal hairpin-shaped frame. As a lace form, this was very popular in the nineteenth century and was often called Maltese lace.

These frames or *forks* may be purchased or made by bending a 350 mm (14 in.) piece of heavy wire into a U shape. A clip across the open end will stabilise the frame and keep the sides parallel. A piece of wood or dowelling with two holes can be made for this purpose, see figure 94.

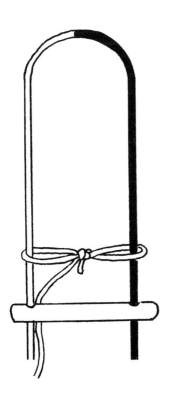
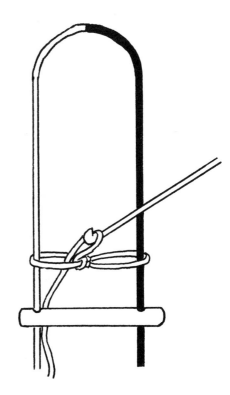

Figure 94a and b

The length of the hairpin frame should be slightly longer than a crochet hook, as the hook passes through the frame during the construction of the braid. If the frame should be shorter, the hook has to be withdrawn repeatedly from the worked frame on one side of the hairpin and re-inserted in the same chain on the other side. The width of the hairpin braid is controlled by the distance between the parallel arms of the frame.

METHOD OF WORKING

Hairpin crochet braids consist of a crochet construction always worked in the centre, and loops which are formed when the yarn goes around the hairpin. This combination gives the braid its charm and character.

To start, make a loop around the outside of the hairpin. Divide this loop into two, with a knot at the centre, The free end of the yarn should always be away from the worked centre, hanging at the back of the frame, see figures 94a and b. Hold the frame at its base with one hand, the crochet hook in the other.

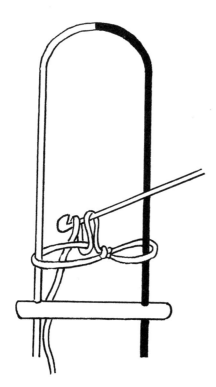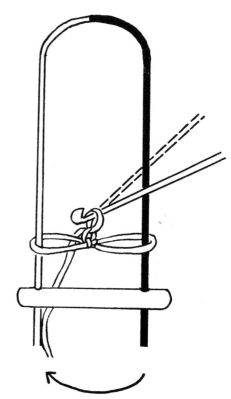

Figure 94c and d

Crochet stitches are always worked in the left-hand loop only. The stitch is worked first on one side of the frame; then, with a left half turn of the hairpin frame, it is worked on the opposite side, which has now the new position of being the left-hand loop. As the construction grows, the frame being turned continuously to the left, the completed braid increases in bulk at the bottom of the frame. It is possible to release a section of the finished work by removing the clip, but do remember to replace it.

The usual stitch to work with hairpin crochet is a double crochet, as shown in the series of drawings. Figures 94e, f and g show the repeating process once the braid has been started and the hairpin turned a left half turn.

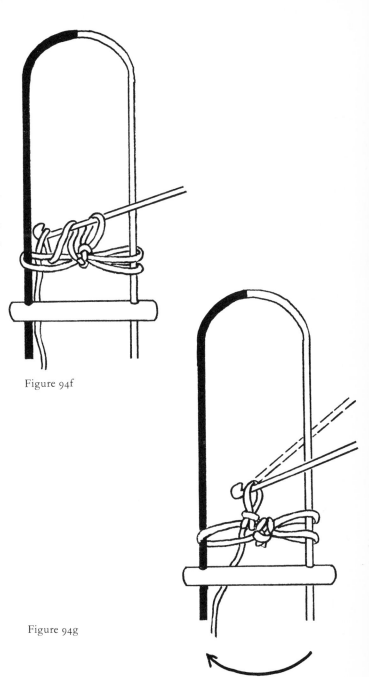

Figure 94f

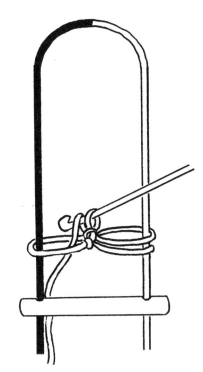

Figure 94e

Figure 94g

Variations can be made to the crochet centre of hairpin crochet braids by substituting any of the crochet stitches, or a combination of stitches, always working in the left-hand loop, see figures 95 and 96.

A thicker spiral braid can be made using the hairpin crochet technique simply by turning the frame three or five half turns instead of one, see figure 97. The hook is then inserted into a left-hand loop made up of three or five threads.

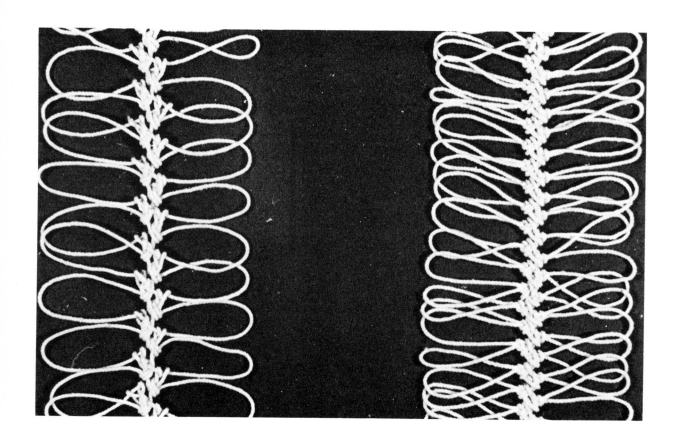

Figure 95   Hairpin crochet with the centre worked in a treble stitch (left) and with a double crochet stitch (right)

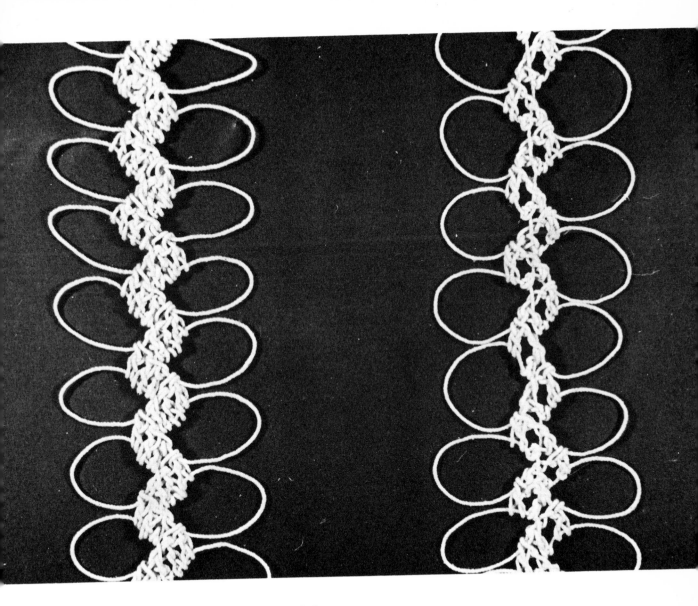

Figure 96 Hairpin crochet with the centre worked with three trebles (left) and with one treble, two chains and one treble (right)

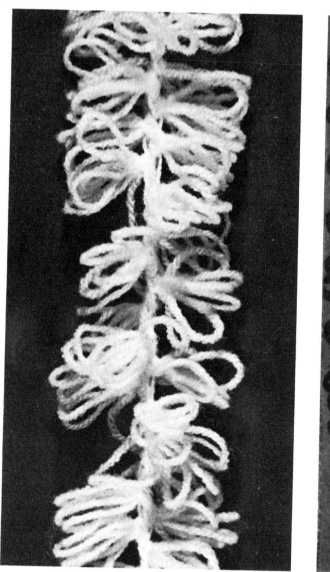

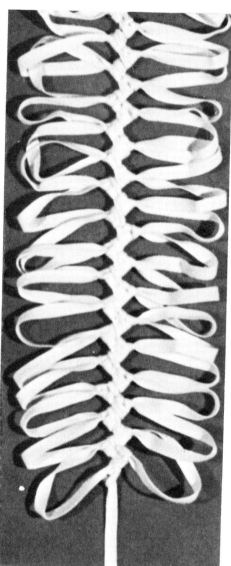

Figure 97 Hairpin crochet braid: the frame is turned three half turns before working the centre

Figure 98

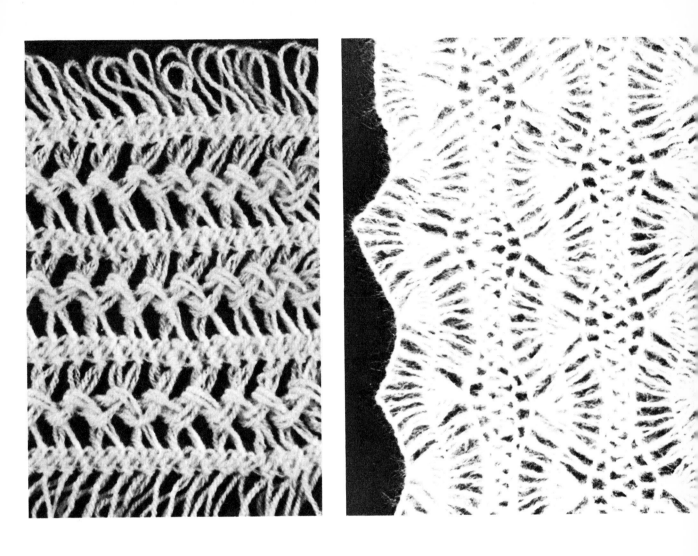

Figure 99 Hairpin crochet fabric: the looped edges are interlinked in pairs

Figure 100 A white mohair scarf made of hairpin crochet strips joined with other crochet stitches, by Marilyn Blunt

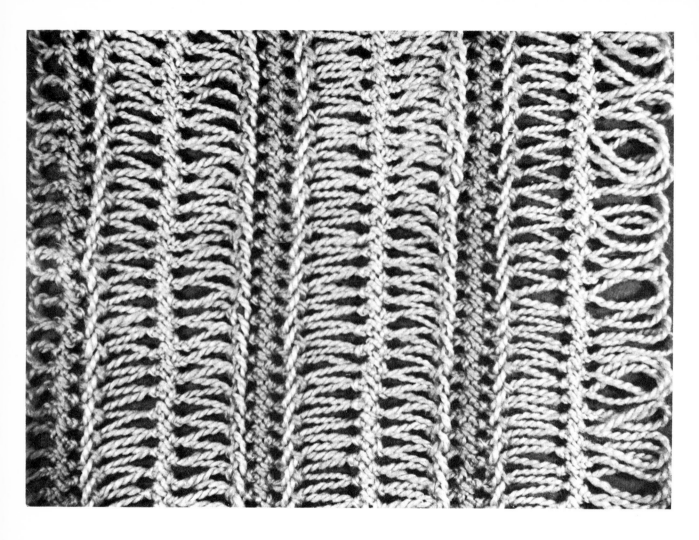

Figure 101 Hairpin crochet fabric worked on two frames in two tones of orange wool. The looped edges are interlinked

Figure 102   Hairpin crochet hanging 710 mm × 710 mm
(24 in. × 24 in.) by June Barker

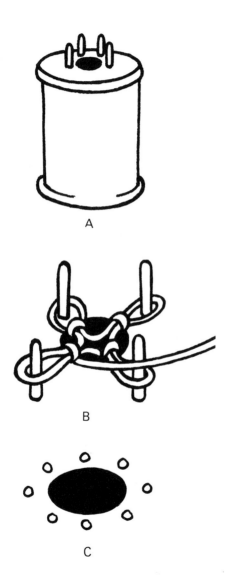

A

B

C

Figure 103   Ring peg or French knitting

Knitting is the best known of all textile construction techniques. Perhaps because of its familiarity it is overlooked as a way of making braids. Knitting is a looping construction worked with a continuous yarn. It can be worked horizontally or in a tubular form.

CIRCULAR KNITTING
(TUBULAR CONSTRUCTION)

Knitting around frames or rings of various diameters is a very old idea and was popular in the past for making cords, caps, bags, purses and scarves. Ring peg or french knitting, using an old wooden cotton reel with a ring of small pins or nails set round the top, as in figure 103a, is a favourite with young children. Tubular knitting is the obvious way to knit a cord or fine braid, using a spool or frame.

To begin, loop the thread over one of the nails and push the loose end of the thread down through the centre hole of the spool. Make loops around each nail or peg in turn, by twisting the thread. The free end of the yarn is then carried round the outside of each nail in turn, see figure 103b. Using a needle or fine crochet hook, the first made loop (or lower one) is lifted over the nail, leaving the new loop in its place. This is one plain knitted stitch. As the work is continued round each peg in turn, a column of tubular knitting is constructed and drops down through the central hole.

The thickness of the knitted tubular braid not only depends on the thread chosen but on the size, number and spacing of the nails. Different spools or frames can be made, some with a larger central hole and with an increased number of nails set around the hole (figure 103c). The spools or frames should be light and easy to hold.

A firm, thick, knitted cord can be worked if a padding cord, or group of threads, is allowed to work down the centre hole as the knitting is worked. By organising different coloured or textured threads in the knitting, many intriguing patterned braids can be made. Tie-dyed threads can be used most effectively in this simple method of knitting a rounded braid.

Figure 104 Tubular knitting

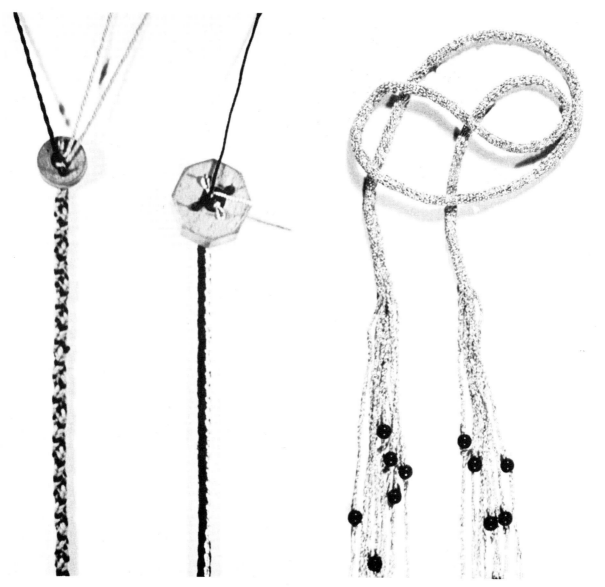

Figure 105 Tubular knitting with four pins and two yarns (right) and two pins and three yarns of different colours (left)

Figure 106 Belt worked in tubular knitted gold fingering, with plaited ends and beads

A knotted rug worked by Ann Rogers in 6 ply rug wool. ▶ (1.52 m [5 ft] diameter)

The more usual form of knitting consists of working horizontally with two needles, one row of stitches being formed upon another. The number of stitches cast onto the needle can be either the width or length of the knitted braid. The number of stitches per centimetre or inch will vary according to the size of the needles, the thickness of the yarn and the firmness of the braid required. Knowledge of the two basic stitches, plain and purl, is sufficient to create simple braids. For more intricate patterns and stitches, consult any knitting manual.

If beads or sequins are used, they must be threaded onto the yarn in the required order, or sequence of colour, before the yarn is used to cast on the stitches. The beads can then be slipped up the yarn and secured in position with the knitted construction, see figures 107 and 108.

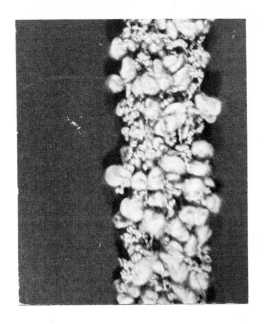

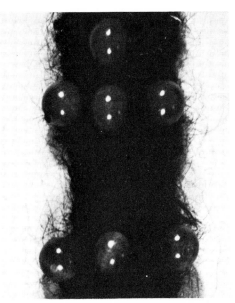

Figure 107 *(above)*   Plain knitting with textured yarn

Figure 108 *(below)*   Plain knitting in black mohair wool, with beads

8 Knotted braids

Knotting has developed from a purely functional form into a decorative one, often known as *macramé*. Macramé is an Arabic word meaning *fringe*, but it is now associated with decorative knotted work. At the moment macramé is enjoying a revival, the last took place in the mid-nineteenth century.

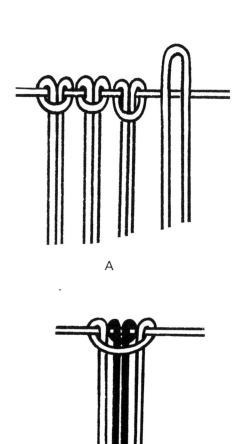

A

B

Figure 109

YARN

All the yarns used for knotting must be easy running, strong, smooth and well twisted. Being a true knotting technique, the yarns are measured in lengths (either the knotting yarn or the foundation thread around which the knots are worked). The knotting lengths are generally four times the finished length, but this is only an approximation, as it does not take into consideration the individual tension of the worker or the arrangement of the knots. The only exact way to calculate the knotting lengths is to work a sample with a measured amount of yarn. From this you will be able to calculate the amount for the completed braid.

The lengths can be arranged to hang from a cord as in figure 109a, fixed to a firm support, such as a hook, door or drawer knob, or even the legs of an upturned chair.

KNOTS

The basic knots are the square knot and the half-hitch and they can be worked to form narrow braids. The knots are formed around a central core, or foundation threads (the shaded area in figure 109b). The width of the braid is determined by the thickness of the hidden core. The length of the foundation threads is the length of the braid. Foundation

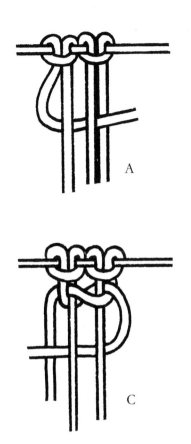
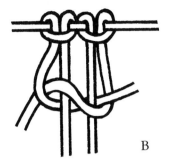
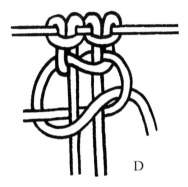

Figure 110 The square knot

threads are never used to form a knot itself.

The square knot, see figure 110, sometimes called the *flat knot*, is worked with two knotting lengths around a foundation thread or threads. The working movements are the same from both sides and are worked alternately. The left side knotting length is positioned behind the central foundation threads, and in front of the knotting length on the right, forming a loop, see figure 110a.

The right knotting length is picked up and, passing over the foundation threads, is threaded through the loop (figure 110b). The two knotting lengths have changed positions.

The knot must be firmly tightened with an even pull on both knotting lengths. To complete the knot, this action is repeated, starting with the length on the right, see figures 110c and d.

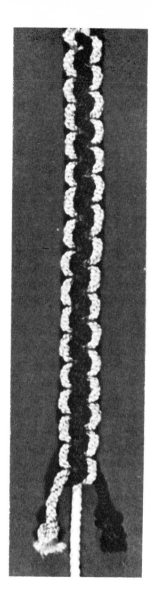

Figure 111　Square knot worked in leather thonging

Figure 112　Square knot worked in two colours (left) and the reverse side (right)

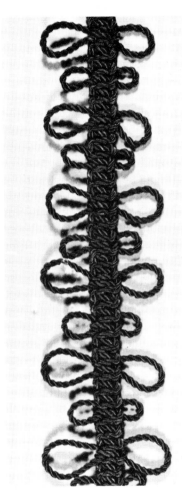

Figure 113 Square knot with picots

Figure 114 Half square knot worked from left side

The square knot can be worked with two different coloured yarns, making two distinctive patterns, one facing the worker and one on the opposite side, see figures 112a and b. If the square knot is worked at intervals down the foundation threads, and then pushed close together, loops or *picots* are formed at

the edge of the braid, see figure 113.

Half square knots can be worked to form twisted columns, the working movements being either a and b *or* c and d in figure 110. If half knots are always worked from the left (a and b), the resulting column will twist to the left and vice versa.

The half-hitch knot, see figure 115, is sometimes referred to as the *buttonhole knot*. It is worked around a foundation thread or threads and may be done with one knotting length always working from the same side; or with two lengths working from alternate sides. Half-hitches worked with one knotting length produce a twisting knotted braid, the twist turning in the same direction as the side from which it is worked.

The knot itself is worked by passing the knotting length in front of and around the foundation threads, then through its own loop. The knot is tightened to form itself around the central core. This is one natural half-hitch.

A reverse half-hitch knot is worked in the same way, but passing *behind* and around the central core. The natural and reverse half-hitch knots are always worked as a pair and in that order. See figure 115. Variations are made by working a series of knots first from the left side and then from the right.

The knots so far described are all suitable for making narrow braids. Double width braids result when two knotted columns are worked with the inside knotting lengths interlinked or interchanged. For wider braids, more lengths are required—they are all knotting lengths. To space them out and to establish the width of the braid, one or two rows of *horizontal cording* should be worked.

Figure 115a and b   The half-hitch knot

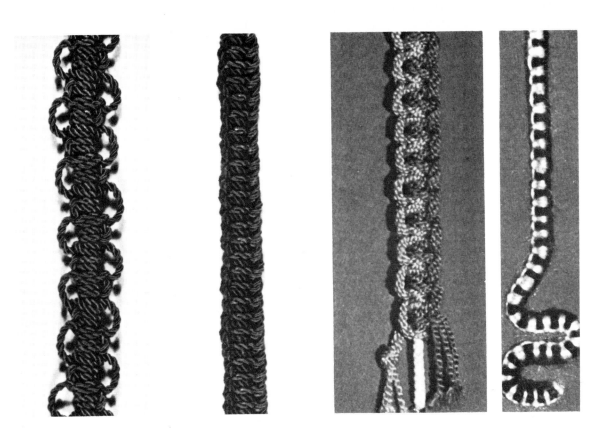

Figure 116 *(left)*   Natural and reverse half-hitch

Figure 117 *(right)*   Natural half-hitch in two colours

Figure 118 *(left)*   Half-hitch in two colours around a foundation thread

Figure 119 *(right)*   Half-hitch: two soft yarns around a rug wool foundation

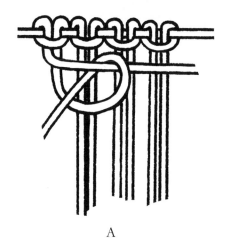

A

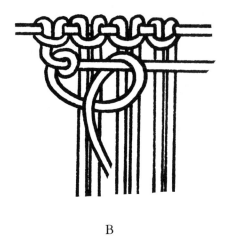

B

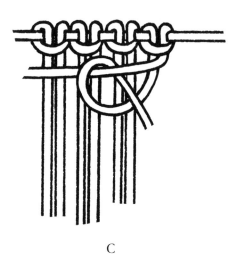

C

D

Figure 120 Cording

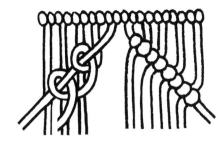

Figure 121 Diagonal cording

Cording is two half-hitch knots worked around a foundation thread. The foundation thread is one of the knotting lengths. It is always held taut and in the direction of the cording. For the horizontal cording, the foundation thread is usually the outside left, or outside right, knotting length, as in figure 120.

The foundation thread or corder is positioned on top of all the other knotting lengths, which in turn are worked with a double half-hitch around them (a and b cording to the right, c and d to the left). It is important that the foundation thread or corder should never knot, all the double half-hitches are formed around it. Cording can also be worked diagonally, with the corder held at an angle.

Any of the knotting lengths can become the corder, see figure 121. All the basic knots can be worked between bands of cording arranged as vertical columns. Or when working in multiples of four, the knotting lengths can be grouped and re-grouped, as in figure 126, to produce a mesh-type fabric.

Figure 122 Patterned cording

89

Figure 123 *(left)*   Cording done in gold fingering

Figure 124 *(right)*   Cording: fine string and wooden beads

Figure 125   Circular cording

Figure 126

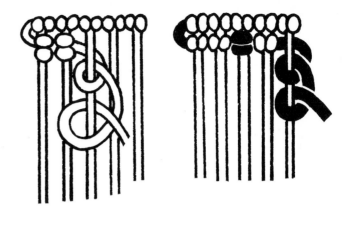

Figure 127 *(left)* Vertical double half-hitch

Figure 128 *(right)* Horizontal and vertical double half-hitch

A vertical double half-hitch can be worked to form two vertical knots as in figure 127. The lengths are never used to form a knot, but each in turn becomes the foundation thread for a long knotting length. The continuous knotting length works horizontally to and fro across the braid. A mixture of cording (horizontal double half-hitches) and vertical double half-hitches can be combined to form patterns as in figures 128 and 129.

Design for patterned braids are easily organised on squared paper, with a horizontal row of squares to represent each length and the vertical rows to represent the rows of worked knots.

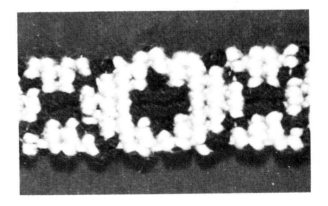

Figure 129 Two-toned patterned cording: horizontal double half-hitch and vertical double half-hitch

The overhand knot, see figure 130, is suitable for making open mesh braids. It can be worked with the other knots or entirely on its own, and the knotting movement can be worked with one or more strands. The lengths for knotting together are held in the fingers at the point just below where the knot is to be formed. The knotting lengths are pulled up and over towards the left and threaded through the loop formed. This loop is then tightened into a knot. For a knotted braid, the lengths can be grouped and re-grouped to form new knots.

Figure 130 *(above left)*   The overhand knot

Figure 131 *(below far left)*

Figure 132 *(below left)*

Figure 133 *(below right)*

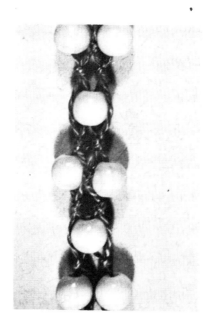

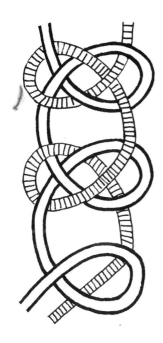

The *Josephine knot*, see figure 134, or *Carrick Bend*, is a flat, figure-of-eight knot formed by two threads or groups of threads. One thread is circled to form a loose ring across the second thread. The second thread is circled in the opposite direction, passing over a thread and under a thread *twice*, to complete the figure-of-eight.

The knot is usually worked from alternate sides to keep the braid flat. Although this is a knotting technique, the two threads must be carefully and evenly tightened. If they are pulled too tight the flat, decorative character of the knot will be lost. If a group of threads are used for this knot, they must all lie flat and in sequence.

Knotted braids can be constructed all with the same knot, or an arrangement and combination of some or all of the knots. The variations are endless, and examples can be seen in figures 136–141.

Figure 134 *(left)*   The Josephine knot

Figure 135 *(above)*   The Josephine knot worked in *Juvisca*

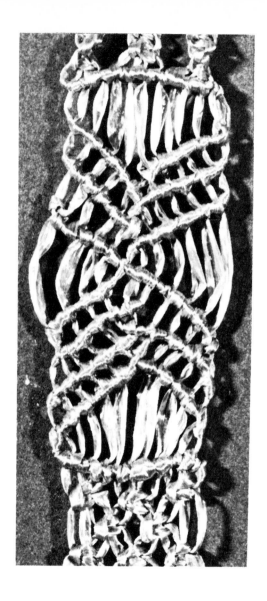

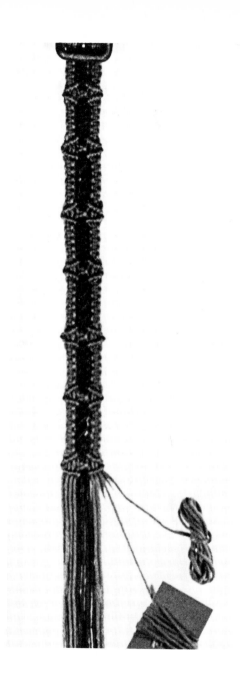

Figure 136   Mixture of knots in raffia

Figure 137   Prevent tangling by tying the ends of the yarn

Figure 138 Knotted centre section and plaited edges

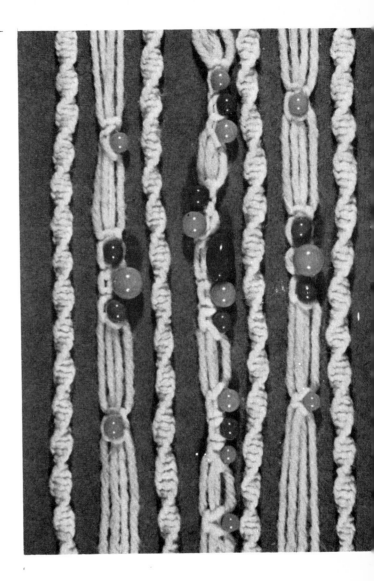

Figure 139 A construction of knotted braids and beads by Paula Burton

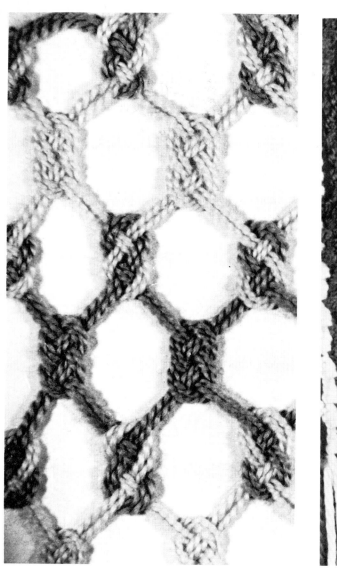

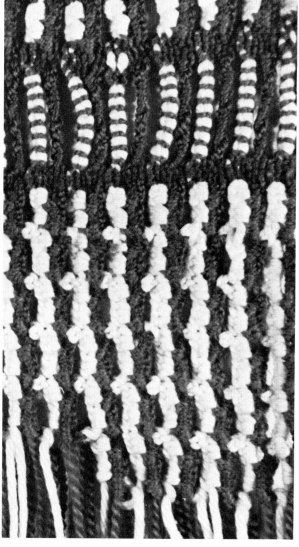

Figure 140 Josephine knot: fabric worked in orange and yellow tapestry wool

Figure 141 Knotted fabric by Sharma Sharif

9 Tatting

Tatting is a knotting technique, thought to have originated in the Near East. It was extremely popular in the eighteenth century when it was worked with quite large shuttles to produce a knotted lace usually applied as surface decoration to garments. The work gradually became finer, using a small shuttle with a white thread, and a lace fabric evolved. Most modern tatting results in distinctive, same-sized ovals and circles, see figure 142.

◀ A plaited over dress made by Hilary Guille—Marrett, a first year Dress and Design student

Modern tatting shuttles vary between 50 mm and 75 mm (2 and 3 in.) long. The shuttle consists of two ovals pointed at each end and joined together with a small support in the middle. The yarn is wound round this centre piece, so that the shuttle restricts the thickness of thread it is possible to use.

To break away from the traditional scale of tatting imposed by the shuttle size, try to use yarn in small balls not wound round a shuttle. A ball of yarn, string, or six-ply wool, 50 mm (2 in.) in diameter, is quite manageable. Tatting yarn should be similar to that for all work using a knotting construction, i.e. easy running, smooth, well twisted and fairly strong.

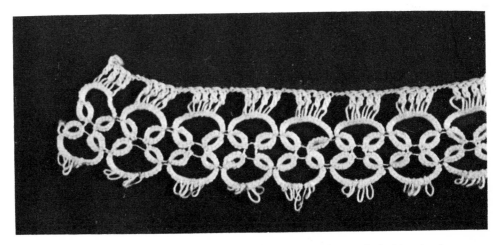

Figure 142   Traditional tatting worked with a shuttle

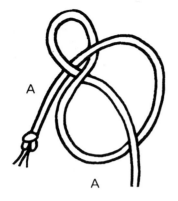

A

A

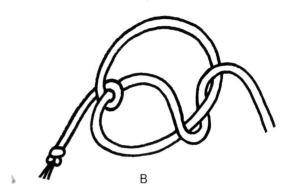

B

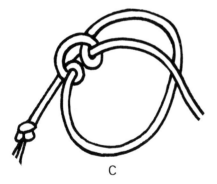

C

Figure 143

METHOD

The tatting knot is made in two parts, an over knot and an under knot. Two half-hitches are used (see also page 86). From a small ball of yarn, make a circle with the yarn. This is usually made around the left hand; the thumb and index finger holding the yarn at point A in figure 143a.

To make the first half-hitch, slip the ball of yarn through the circle, leaving a loop, and back over the top of the circle through its own loop, as shown in figure 143a. On tightening this knot, pull the yarn with a jerk, thus making the knot form from the yarn in the circle, *not* the free yarn running to the ball. The first part of the knot should be formed as in figure 143b, and should be able to slip along the free yarn. Follow this figure to make the second knot (around, under and through the circle of yarn) which is drawn up close to the first knot, where together they make the familiar tatting knot, see figure 143c.

The knotting is repeated until the required number of knots have been formed along the circle of yarn. If the yarn is pulled tight, all the knots made free running on the yarn will come together in a tight circle, the basic feature of all tatting work. Another circle can then be formed and worked.

The simplest form of decoration in tatting is to work picots. Picots or loops are made by leaving a space between the worked knots which when pulled together, make a looped edge. By working a number of circles or half circles one after another, a tatting braid is produced, see figure 144.

Figure 144   Tatting with a thick cotton cord

Wrapped braids are extremely easy to make and require very little skill. This form of construction for a braid should not be overlooked merely because of its simplicity.

The braid is worked by wrapping a decorative yarn over and under two foundation cords in a figure-of-eight movement, as shown in figures 145 and 146. The thicker foundation cords are completely covered by the wrapped construction. All the yarns can be kept in balls and released when required. This avoids any joins in the hidden foundation yarns which can give the braid an uneven appearance.

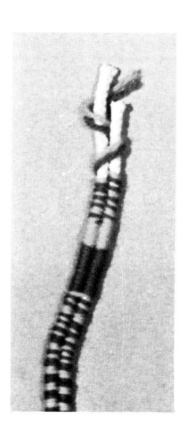

Figure 145

Figure 146   Wrapped braid as shown in figure 145 with two yarns used as one

Figure 147

Figure 148 Wrapped braid as shown in figure 146. White piping cord forms the foundation thread, wrapped with navy blue piping cord

Variations can be made either in the working yarn used in the figure-of-eight movement, or by altering the foundation yarns. One very thick foundation cord, paired with a fine one, produces an interesting moulded braid. A wider braid can be formed using a number of foundation cords, but keeping the same wrapped construction.

This type of braid is very flexible and can be worked to form angles and curves. As a rug-making technique worked with rug wool, grasses or strips of cotton, the braid is sewn or wrapped together, usually into a large oval or round shape, at the same time as the braid construction.

A more decorative wrapped braid is shown in figures 147 and 148. Two wrapped yarns are used, one working from the right-hand side of the foundation cords, the other from the left, which together make a figure-of-eight. This braid is usually worked so that the two foundation cords are seen at regular intervals along the length of the braid.

Figure 149 Section of scarf fabric: wrapped technique, beads,
edged with tablet woven braids by Helen Radcliffe

Needleweaving is the simplest form of weaving, and is highly suitable for making braids. The only equipment needed is a large-eyed needle, preferably with a blunt end. The warp or foundation lengths of yarn hang vertically, being the length of the woven braid. The width of the braid depends on the number and thickness of the warp strands in the length.

To needleweave, the warp strands are pulled taut and a needle threaded with a weft thread or filling yarn is made to go over and under each strand in turn, as in darning, see figure 150. On the next row, the action is reversed. A comb or fork can be used to keep the taut warp lengths evenly spaced. It is important to pull the weft yarn evenly at the end of each row, as this decides the width and density of the braid. Using the shaft of the needle, each weft row can be pushed into position, keeping it horizontal. If desired, the weft can be packed so tightly that all the warp strands are hidden, making a very dense braid.

Simple variations can be made in the woven construction by altering the number of strands that the needle is made to go over or under. If these become very complex, then it is easier to make the braid on a four- or eight-shaft loom.

Figure 150   Needleweaving, showing density of weft

Figure 151 Needleweaving, without a needle, using leather thonging

Figure 152 Fabric made from needlewoven braids sewn together, by Sonia Robinson

Figure 153 First year students' group project: needlewoven
braids used as the weft for a wall hanging 457 mm × 710 mm
(18 in. × 24 in.)

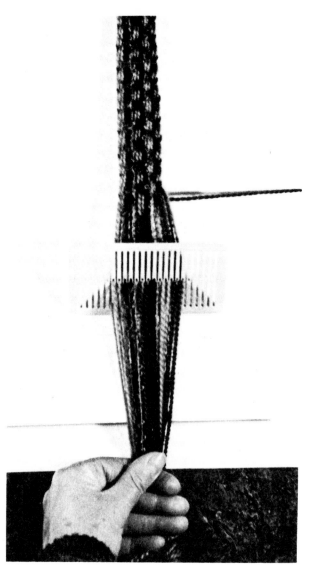

THE HOLE AND SLOT HEDDLE

For plain weaving, a simple and inexpensive piece of equipment is a metal hole and slot heddle, see figure 154. Each warp length is threaded either through a hole or slot. By pushing down or pulling up the heddle, the two openings or sheds are formed for the weft, eliminating the darning action. The warp lengths must be chosen from yarns that will pass easily through the holes and slots.

TAPE OR BRAID LOOMS

Old tape or braid looms have a hole and slot construction at one end of a small rectangular box. The box is kept static on a table and the warp is lifted or lowered to produce the alternate sheds. The braid is woven beyond the heddle end. At the opposite end there is a roller around which the spare warp is wound. The warp is released at intervals as the braiding progresses.

Figure 154   Hole and slot heddle

Figure 155   Old braid loom

TEXTILE JEWELRY

Figure 156 *(left)*   Choker, made from an eight-stranded round
plait mounted on an alice band

Figure 157 *(right)*   Choker, a needlewoven band, with the ends
finished by plaiting and knotting

TEXTILE CONSTRUCTION PICTURES

The following pictures are the result of a project with first-year dress and design students. The brief was to use as wide a range as possible of all the textile construction techniques described in this book. The small areas of textiles were worked separately and applied to a backing sheet of tarlatan or hessian, stretched over a simple wooden frame.

Figure 158 *(left)*   Linda Elphick

Figures 159, 160, 161 and 162 *(opposite)*   From left to right: Hilary Guille-Marrett, Jackie Garrett, Jenny Lund, Paula Burton

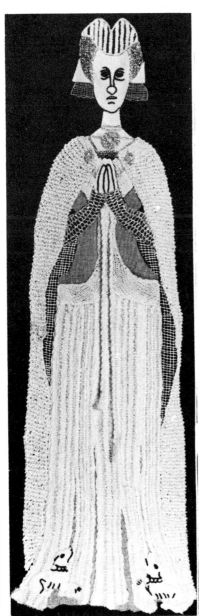

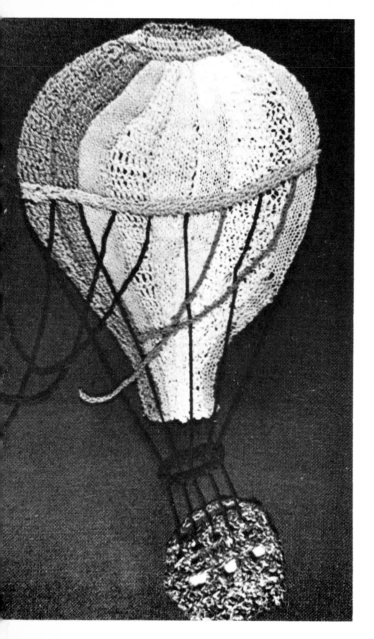

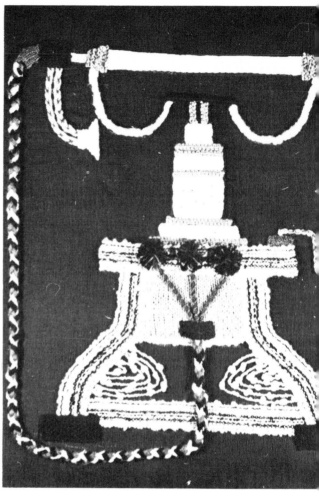

Figure 163 *(left)*   Janet Blemmings

Figure 164 *(right)*   Pauline Oddy

Bibliography

The Textile Arts, Vera Birrell, Harper and Row

Anchor Manual of Needlework, J. and P. Coats, Batsford London, Branford Newton Centre, Massachusetts

Encyclopaedia of Needlework, Thérèse de Dillmont, D.M.C. Library

The Ashley Book of Knots, Clifford W. Ashley, Faber London

Encyclopaedia of Knots and Fancy Rope Work, Raoul Graumont and John Hensel, Cornell Maritime Press

Textiles of Ancient Peru and Their Techniques, Raoul d'Harcourt, University of Washington Press

Byways in Hand Weaving, Mary Meigs Attwater, Macmillan

The Weavers' Craft, L. E. Simpson and M. Weir, Dryad, Leicester

Mary Thomas's Book of Knitting Patterns, Hodder and Stoughton London

Introducing Macramé, Eirian Short, Batsford London, Watson-Guptill New York

Macramé: The Art of Creative Knotting, Virginia Harvey, Van Nostrand Reinhold New York

Creative Textile Craft, Rolf Hartung, Batsford London, Van Nostrand Reinhold New York

The History of Needlework Tools and Accessories, Sylvia Groves, *Country Life*

Needleweaving, Edith John, Batsford London, Branford Newton Centre, Massachusetts

Suppliers

Most large stores and needlecraft shops will offer a variety of yarns, cords, tapes and strings; knitting needles, crochet hooks and hairpin forks.

Yarns
J. Hyslop Bathgate, Victoria Works, Galashiels, Scotland
   Wool yarns, plain and fancy
Hugh Griffiths, Brookdale, 11 Frome Road, Beckington, Bath, Somerset
   Fancy cotton yarns, raffine, cords, *Juvisca* braid
T. M. Hunter, Sutherland, Wool Mill, Brora, Scotland
Tulloch of Scotland Ltd, Lerwick, Scotland
   2-ply Shetland wool
Robert Ladislaw & Sons, Seafield Mills, Keith, Scotland
J. & W. Stuart Ltd, Esk Mills, Musselburgh, Scotland

Inkle looms and tablets
Dryad, Northgates, Leicester
Harris Looms, Grove Road, Hawkhurst, Kent

Beads
Sesame Ventures, Greenham Hall, Wellington, Somerset

General suppliers
Dryad, Northgates, Leicester

The Needlewoman Shop, 146 Regent Street, London W1
Art Needlework Industries Ltd, 7 St Michael's Mansions, Ship Street, Oxford
Nottingham Handicraft Company, Melton Road, West Bridgeford, Nottingham NG2 6HD

USA

Yarns
Bucky King Embroideries Unlimited, 121 South Drive, Pittsburgh, Pennsylvania 15238
American Thread Corporation, 90 Park Avenue, New York

General suppliers
Local suppliers may be discovered through the Yellow Pages of the telephone directory, under such headings as *Art and Craft Supplies*

Mail Order
American Handicraft Company, 20 West 14th Street, New York